MW01118192

TO: *Cassie*

FROM: *Lori*

Design by Anderson Thomas Design

Published by C.R. Gibson®
C.R. Gibson® is a registered trademark of Thomas Nelson, Inc.
Nashville, Tennessee 37214

Printed in Mexico.

ISBN 0-7667-6651-9
GB647R

Babies Are A Special Gift

photographs by
KIM ANDERSON

poetry by
PAULA FINN

CONGRATULATIONS
to a special couple!

May your new baby grow in

the best of health,

to a life of greatest joy;

to be a proud reflection of you,

of all the goodness in your lives and

all the love in your hearts.

Are you ready
to begin a journey
that is indescribable to those
who have never traveled it –
a journey filled with wonder,
c h a l l e n g e ,
and abundant joy?

Are you ready to recall the
e n c h a n t m e n t
of the world you knew as a child,
where stars were for wishing,
snowflakes were for tasting,
and butterflies were
for chasing?

Are you ready to experience a miracle?

Because, as new parents - you will.

To become a parent is to begin a journey

where the challenges are sometimes

the greatest –

and the rewards are

always the richest.

You worry
whether the baby's room
is complete, and if the house is
well-stocked with crib and cradle,
blankets and booties . . .

You wonder
if you know enough about parenting –
if you've talked to enough people,
or read enough books . . .

You wonder
if you'll ever have a social
life again, and how
you'll adjust . . .

Yet from the first moment you see and hold your baby,

you will feel an indescribable love and connection –

a n d   y o u   w i l l   b e   r e a d y.

THE BIRTH OF A NEW BABY
is a new beginning.

It's a time of new dreams,

new emotions, new roles,

new routines, new pleasures,

new adventures, and most of all,

n e w   l o v e . . .

A love that is natural and selfless,

and unlike any other.

Babies can

open our eyes to a new world of beauty,

our minds to a new world of promise,

and our hearts to a new world of love.

Babies need

parents with patience, creativity, humor,

fairness, wisdom, strength, compassion,

gentleness, understanding.

Babies need parents like you.

WHAT A BEAUTIFUL LITTLE FACE!

It's the most beautiful face you've ever seen.

What *p e r f e c t* little hands!

They're the most adorable

hands you've ever seen.

Babies can bring joy to your heart,

life to your dreams –

and so much *m e a n i n g* to your life.

May you find

the strength to protect without

s m o t h e r i n g ,

the wisdom to guide without

c o n t r o l l i n g ,

the compassion to listen without

j u d g i n g ,

the faith to encourage without

p u s h i n g ,

the love to cherish without

p o s s e s s i n g .

May you follow

your heart in guiding your child,

and believe in yourself,

KNOWING

k n o w i n g

that you can solve the problems

and survive the pressures that

parenting often brings.

And may you find in each new day

a   c h a n c e   t o   s h a r e   y o u r   l o v e .

A PARENT'S LOVE

is accepting, supportive, tender,

respectful, forgiving.

A parent's love is forever.

May your baby awaken

you to fond memories,

inspire you to new dreams,

and open you to new joys.

Watching your baby grow can deepen your faith in miracles,

and your appreciation for life in all its goodness and beauty.

PARENTING MAY BRING

occasional sorrows, frustrations, and hurt feelings,

but you will find your joy will outweigh your sorrows,

your rewards will outnumber your frustrations,

and your love will sustain you.

You will find that this new little life

is your most precious creation.

Each day,
your baby grows stronger,
smarter, bigger.

Each day,
your baby grows in
awareness, confidence, curiosity,
and in all the qualities
that make your baby
u n i q u e .

AND AS YOUR BABY GROWS…
your love will grow even more.

The nicest things come in small packages – wrapped in joy,

filled with goodness, and sent with love.

A BABY'S WORLD

is fresh and vibrant,

where the grass is soft and the sun is

warm and soothing –

where colors look richer,

blossoms smell sweeter,

and the music of happiness fills the air.

TO RAISE A CHILD

is to be part of a miracle,

and no matter how often

you hold a small hand in yours,

or tie a tiny shoe,

or hear a young voice in prayer . . .

it will never be enough.

Welcome to your Little One!

May your baby's path be blessed

with health and happiness . . .

and a lifetime of

d r e a m s   c o m e   t r u e .